FILM MUSIC

FOR SOLO PIANO

CHESTER MUSIC
part of The Music Sales Group

London / New York / Paris / Sydney / Copenhagen / Berlin / Madrid / Tokyo

Published by:
Chester Music
8/9 Frith Street, London W1D 3JB, England.

Exclusive Distributors:
Music Sales Limited
Distribution Centre, Newmarket Road, Bury St Edmunds,
Suffolk IP33 3YB, England.
Music Sales Pty Limited
120 Rothschild Avenue, Rosebery, NSW 2018, Australia.

Order No. CH67804
ISBN 1-84449-343-1
This book © Copyright 2003 by Chester Music.

Compiled by Heather Ramage and Nick Crispin.
Music processed by Note-orious Productions Limited.
Aberdeen arranged by Alastair Cameron.
C'est Le Vent, Betty; *Prelude/Main Theme from The Belles Of St Trinian's*;
Autumn In Connecticut; *The Departure*; *Anna's Theme*; *Reprise*;
Theme from Somewhere In Time and *Alicia Vive* arranged by Jack Long.
Cover design by Fresh Lemon.
Photographs courtesy of Ronald Grant Archive.
Printed in Malta by Interprint Limited.

Your Guarantee of Quality
As publishers, we strive to produce every book to the highest commercial standards.
The music has been freshly engraved and the book has been carefully designed
to minimise awkward page turns and to make playing from it a real pleasure.
Particular care has been given to specifying acid-free, neutral-sized
paper made from pulps which have not been elemental chlorine bleached.
This pulp is from farmed sustainable forests and was produced
with special regard for the environment.
Throughout, the printing and binding have been planned to ensure
a sturdy, attractive publication which should give years of enjoyment.
If your copy fails to meet our high standards, please inform us and
we will gladly replace it.

www.musicsales.com

Aberdeen *from Aberdeen* . . . . ZBIGNIEW PREISNER 4

Alicia Vive *from Talk To Her* . . . . ALBERTO IGLESIAS 89

All Love Can Be *from A Beautiful Mind* . . . . JAMES HORNER 9

Anna's Theme *from The Red Violin* . . . . JOHN CORIGLIANO 57

Autumn In Connecticut *from Far From Heaven* . . . . ELMER BERNSTEIN 34

Le Banquet *from Amelie* . . . . YANN TIERSEN 6

Beetlejuice *from Beetlejuice* . . . . DANNY ELFMAN 12

C'est Le Vent, Betty *from Betty Blue* . . . . GABRIEL YARED 15

Chronicle Scherzo *from Citizen Kane* . . . . BERNARD HERRMANN 28

The Departure f*rom Gattaca* . . . . MICHAEL NYMAN 37

Eternal Vow *from Crouching Tiger, Hidden Dragon* . . . . TAN DUN 32

The Heart Asks Pleasure First / The Promise / The Sacrifice
from The Piano . . . . MICHAEL NYMAN 62

The Hours *from The Hours* . . . . PHILIP GLASS 40

Love Theme *from Romeo & Juliet* . . . . NINO ROTA 70

Merry Christmas, Mr Lawrence
from Merry Christmas, Mr Lawrence . . . . RYUICHI SAKAMOTO 50

Murder On The Orient Express
from Murder On The Orient Express . . . . RICHARD RODNEY BENNETT 60

My Father's Favourite *from Sense & Sensibility* . . . . PATRICK DOYLE 73

My Heart Will Go On *from Titanic* . . . . JAMES HORNER 92

Passage Of Time *from Chocolat* . . . . RACHEL PORTMAN 25

Pelagia's Song *from Captain Corelli's Mandolin* . . . . STEPHEN WARBECK 22

Prelude / Main Theme *from The Belles of St Trinian's* . . . SIR MALCOLM ARNOLD 20

Reprise *from Spirited Away* . . . . JOE HISAISHI 78

Theme *from Schindler's List* . . . . JOHN WILLIAMS 66

Theme *from Somewhere In Time* . . . . JOHN BARRY 86

Aberdeen
from Aberdeen

By Zbigniew Preisner

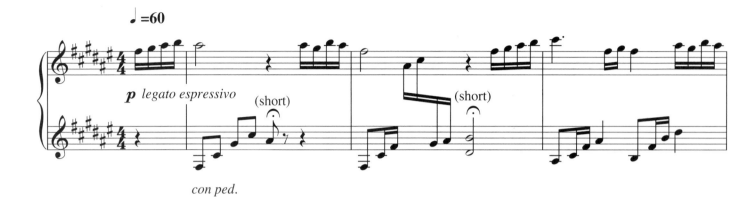

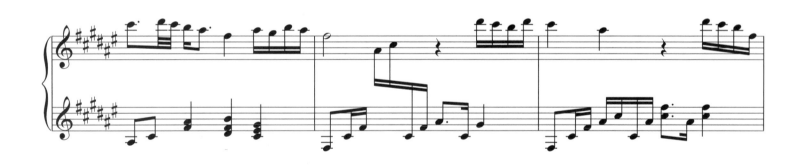

molto rall.

L.H.

dim. - - - - - - - - *p*

5

Le Banquet
from Amelie

By Yann Tiersen

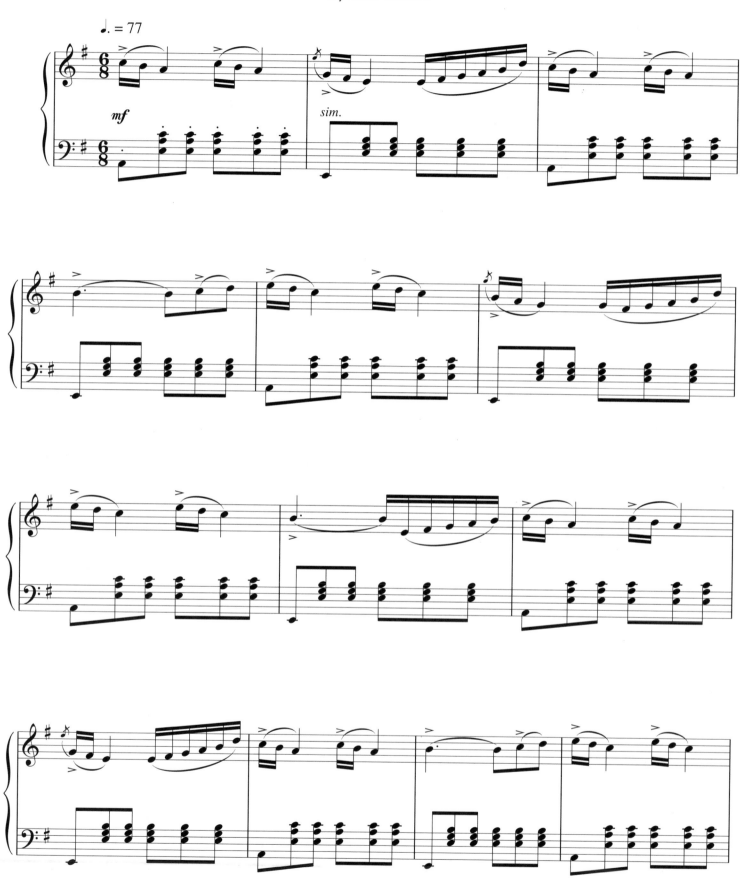

All Love Can Be
from A Beautiful Mind

Words by Will Jennings
Music by James Horner

Beetlejuice
from Beetlejuice

By Danny Elfman

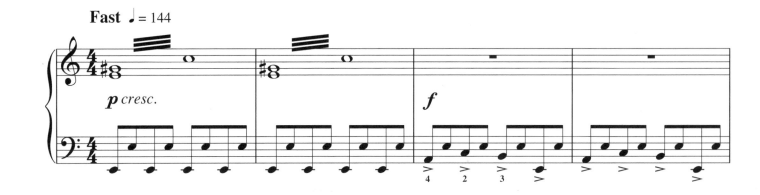

C'est Le Vent, Betty
from Betty Blue

By Gabriel Yared

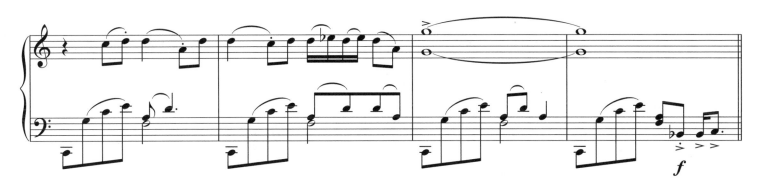

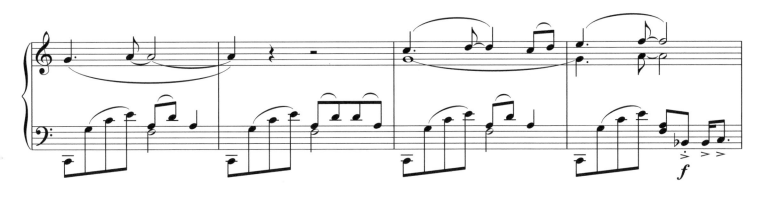

Prelude/Main Theme
from The Belles of St Trinian's

By Sir Malcolm Arnold

Pelagia's Song
from Captain Corelli's Mandolin

By Stephen Warbeck

23

24

Passage Of Time
from Chocolat

By Rachel Portman

Chronicle Scherzo
from Citizen Kane

By Bernard Herrmann

30

D.S. al Coda

Coda

Eternal Vow
from Crouching Tiger, Hidden Dragon

By Tan Dun

♩ = 120 **Freely**

Con pedale

Autumn In Connecticut
from Far From Heaven

By Elmer Bernstein

Poco rubato ♩ = c.54

The Departure
from Gattaca

By Michael Nyman

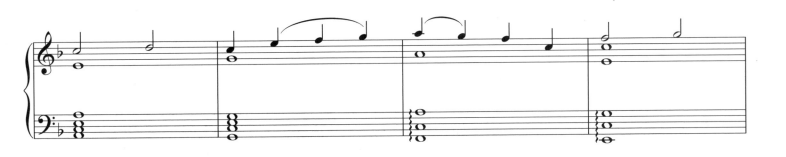

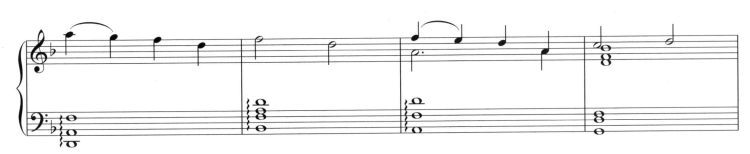

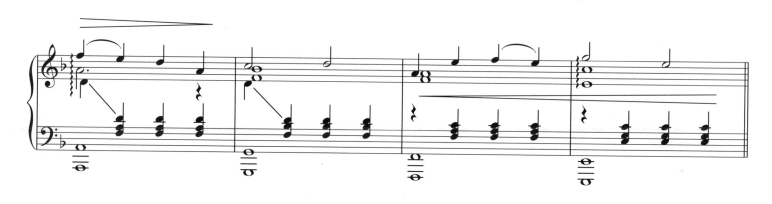

38

The Hours
from The Hours

By Philip Glass

Merry Christmas, Mr Lawrence
from Merry Christmas, Mr Lawrence

Music by Ryuichi Sakamoto

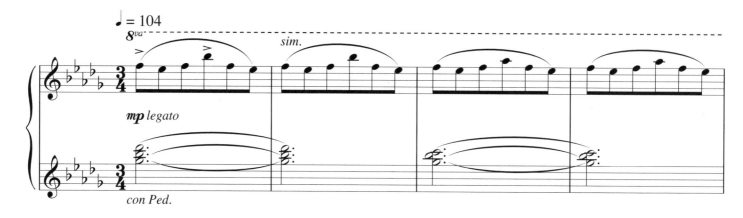

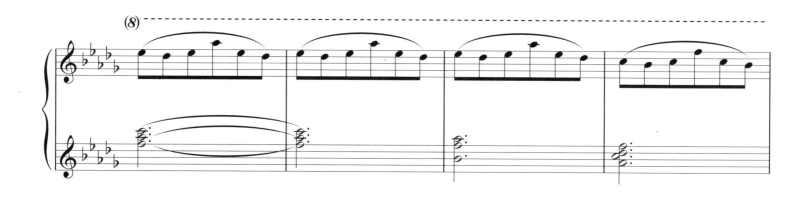

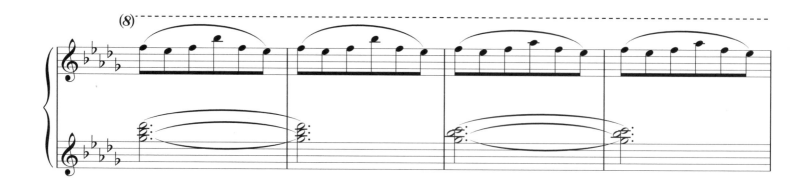

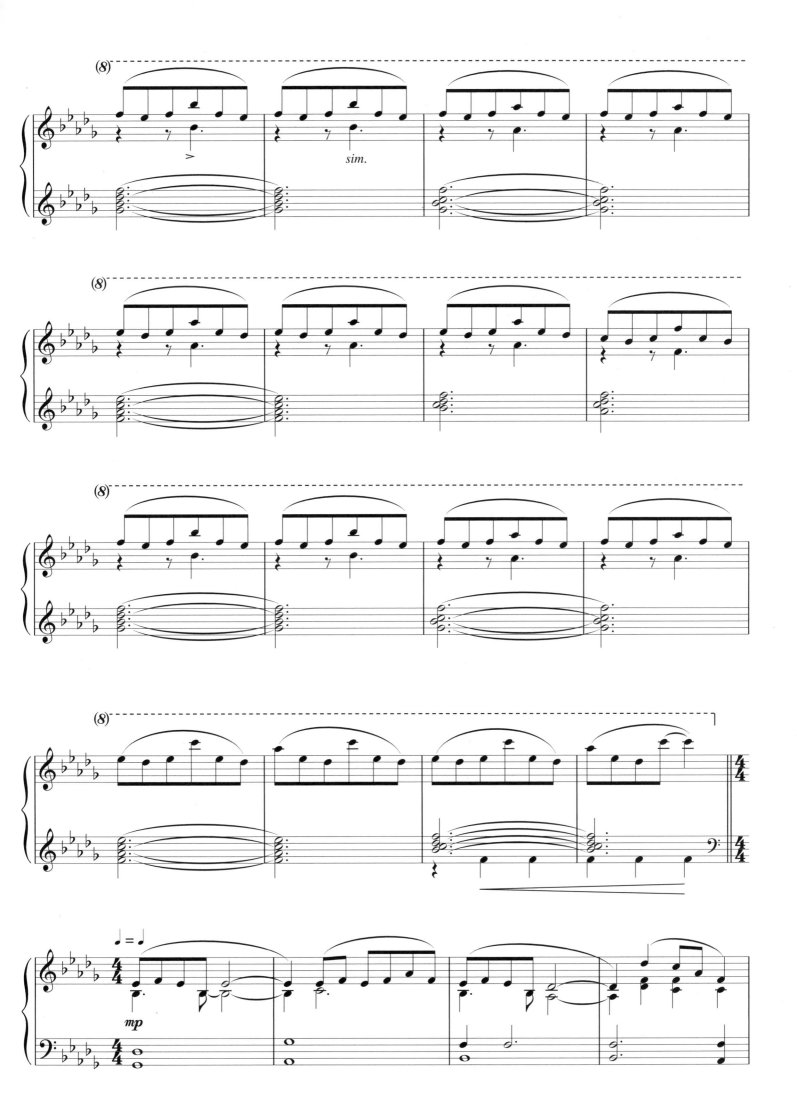

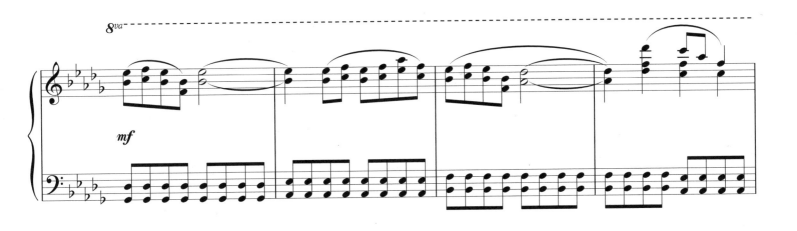

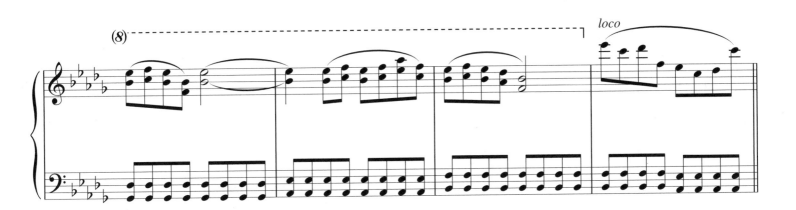

Anna's Theme
from The Red Violin

By John Corigliano

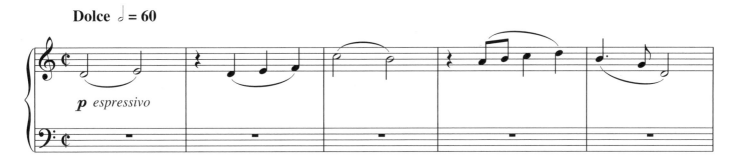

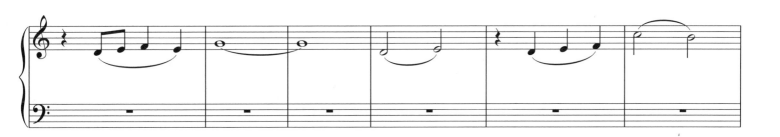

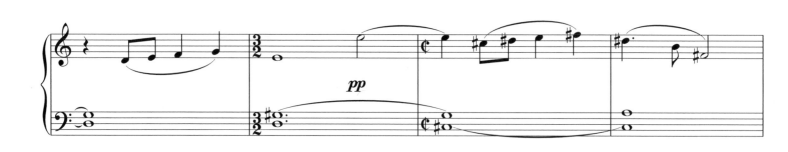

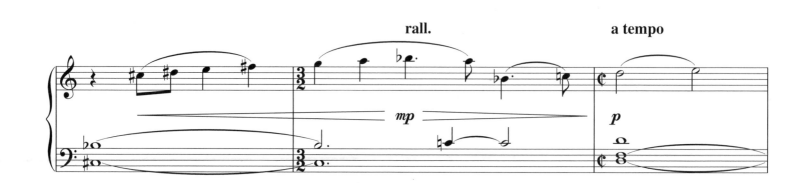

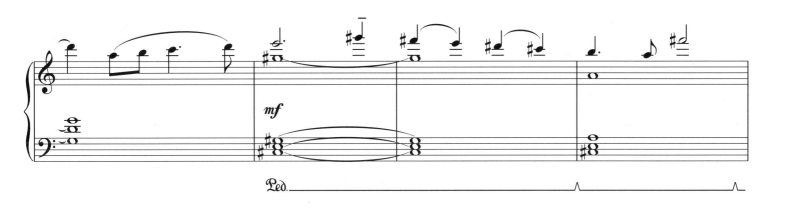

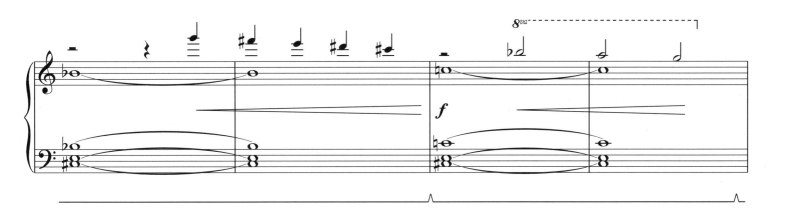

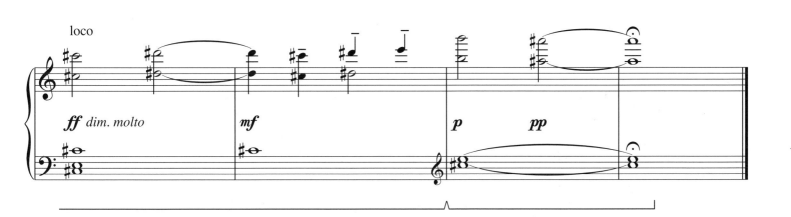

Murder On The Orient Express
from Murder On The Orient Express

By Richard Rodney Bennett

Moderately

To Coda $\oplus$

D.C. al Coda

CODA
$\oplus$

The Heart Asks Pleasure First/
The Promise/The Sacrifice
from The Piano

By Michael Nyman

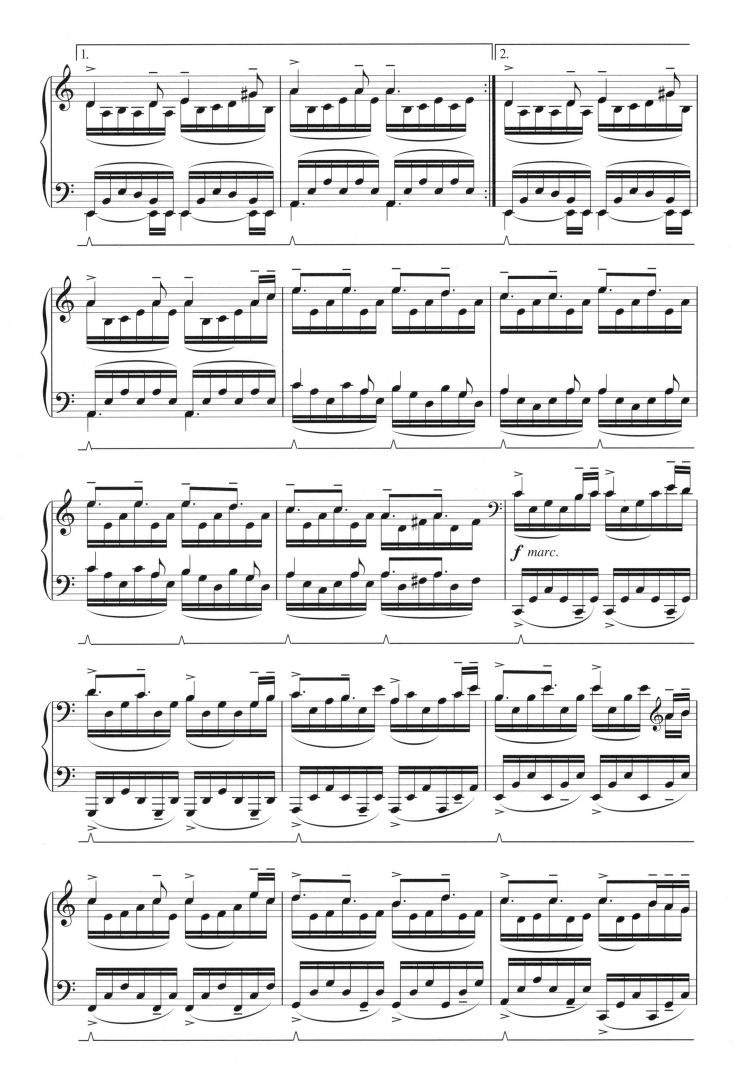

65

Theme
from Schindler's List

By John Williams

Expressively

Love Theme
from Romeo & Juliet

By Nino Rota

Slow and expressive

My Father's Favourite
from Sense & Sensibility

By Patrick Doyle

74

Reprise
from Spirited Away

By Joe Hisaishi

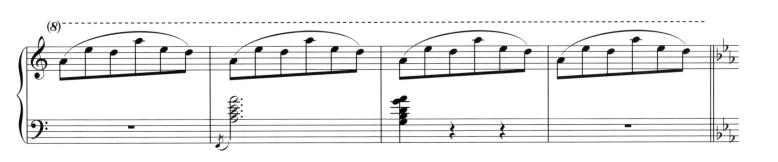

Theme
from Somewhere In Time

By John Barry

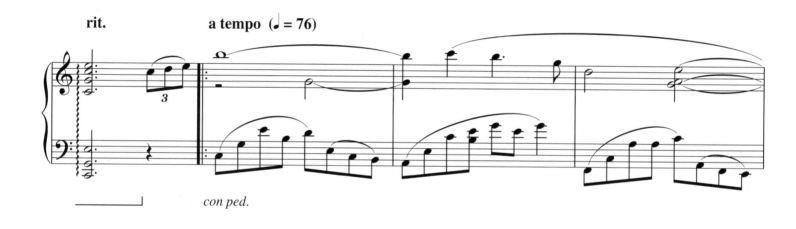

rit.   a tempo, ma poco meno mosso

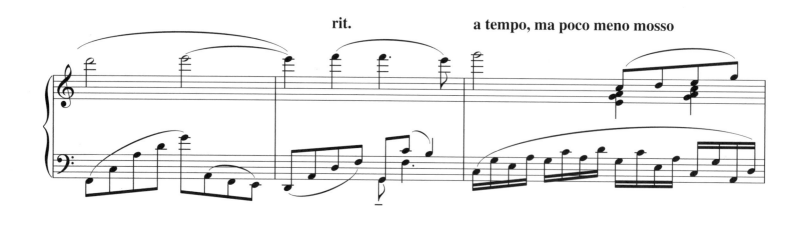

rit.

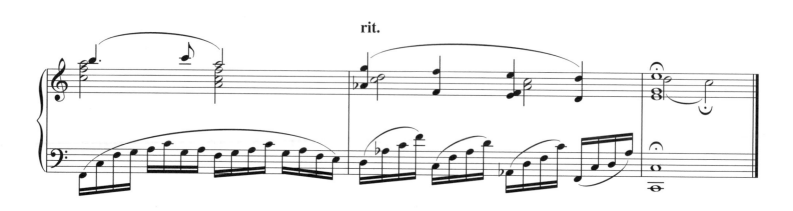

Alicia Vive
from Talk To Her

By Alberto Iglesias